Bag Ladies & Mr. Bojangles: Spiritual Vagabonds in the Church

Apostle Paula Ferguson

Published by FOSA Publishing LLC, 2025.

While every precaution has been taken in the preparation of this book, the publisher assumes no responsibility for errors or omissions, or for damages resulting from the use of the information contained herein.

BAG LADIES & MR. BOJANGLES: SPIRITUAL VAGABONDS IN THE CHURCH

First edition. December 22, 2025.

Copyright © 2025 Apostle Paula Ferguson.

ISBN: 979-8992303971

Written by Apostle Paula Ferguson.

Table of Contents

Why This Book Was Written 1
Introduction: That's Not Even Your Stuff 3
Chapter 1: What's in Your Bag? 9
Chapter 2: Why Are You Even Carrying That? 13
Chapter 3: When the Bow Breaks 17
Chapter 4: Who Packed Your Bag 23
Chapter 5: Are You a Bag Lady or a Mr. Bojangles? 29
Chapter 6: Burdens of Legacy: When the Weight Transfers 35
Chapter 7: Forgiving Others, Forgiving Yourself 39
Chapter 8: The Lighter Load 45
Chapter 9: A Framework for Freedom 49
Chapter 10: The Takers and the Broken 55
Self-Analysis: Identifying the Weight 59
Answer Key 1 65
Answer Key 2 71
Closing Prayer: A Cry for Freedom and Healing 73

Why This Book Was Written

This book was written because so many of us carry things that were never meant to be ours. Burdens, responsibilities, pain, shame, and emotional baggage—we hold onto them as if they define us, but the truth is, they weigh us down and keep us from living the life we were created for.

I've carried my own baggage—more than I care to admit. I was the one crying out on the grassy hill, pleading for someone to hear me, to validate me, to love me. I remember saying, *"Please see me! Please understand me! Please need me because I'm hurting."* That was the weight I carried for far too long. And while I thought I was holding onto it to survive, I realize now it was holding me back from thriving.

As I began to see others in similar situations, I felt compelled to write this book. I saw the **Bag Ladies** and **Mr. Bojangles** of the world, scattered in every corner of life. These were people crying out in silence, carrying invisible baggage everywhere they went. They reminded me of who I used to be.

This isn't just my story—it's all of ours. Every person, whether they realize it or not, carries baggage. It doesn't matter if you're walking through an airport with a carry-on, lugging around multiple suitcases, or just clutching a small backpack—*everyone* has something.

The question is: **Where are you going?**

You can't move forward if your baggage keeps dragging you down. This book was written to help you see the weight you've been carrying, to understand where it came from, and to empower you to let it go. My prayer is that these words help you unpack your burdens, break free from cycles of pain, and step into the healing and purpose God has for your life.

We're not meant to carry it all. We were designed to live lightly, to walk in freedom, and to trust the One who promises to take our burdens and give us rest.

If you're holding on to baggage, know this: you're not alone, and you don't have to stay this way. You can lay it down.

This book is a guide, a testimony, and an encouragement to help you do just that.

With love and a shared understanding,
Paula Ferguson

Introduction: That's Not Even Your Stuff

Let me ask you something: What are you carrying, and why are you still holding onto it?

For many of us in the Christian faith, some of the heaviest bags we carry come from the church itself. They're not just burdens we've picked up along life's journey; they're weights we've inherited from ministry obligations, unresolved church conflicts, or unmet expectations.

Some of us are carrying responsibilities for multiple ministries and departments because others have refused to step up. We've taken on tasks that don't belong to us, convinced ourselves it's for the greater good, and neglected to hold others accountable. This isn't just a practical issue; it's a spiritual one.

Carrying What Wasn't Meant for You

The Bible gives us clear wisdom about carrying burdens—our own and others'. In Galatians 6:2, Paul instructs believers, *"Carry each other's burdens, and in this way you will fulfill the law of Christ."* This scripture highlights the importance of mutual support in the body of Christ. However, Paul also balances this teaching just a few verses later by reminding us, *"Each one should carry their own load"* (Galatians 6:5).

This isn't a contradiction; it's a call to discernment. There's a difference between helping someone bear a burden they cannot carry alone and enabling someone to shirk their responsibilities. As Christians, we're called to serve—but not to the point of exhaustion or resentment. When we overextend ourselves in ministry, taking on more than God intended for us, we risk not only burnout but also disrupting the balance and function of the body of Christ.

The Case of John Mark

The early church wasn't immune to this kind of conflict. In Acts 13, John Mark, a young disciple, accompanied Paul and Barnabas on their first missionary journey. But partway through the trip, John Mark abandoned the mission, returning home to Jerusalem. Later, when Paul and Barnabas were planning a second journey, Barnabas wanted to bring John Mark along again, but Paul refused. This disagreement became so sharp that the two apostles parted ways (Acts 15:36–40).

Why did this happen? Because John Mark had refused to carry his weight the first time. His abandonment caused a rift, and Paul wasn't willing to risk it happening again. This is a powerful example of how unresolved baggage—whether it's fear, immaturity, or irresponsibility—can disrupt relationships and hinder ministry.

The truth is, situations like this still happen in the church today. There are times when people fail to carry their share of the load, leaving others to pick up the slack. And while it's good to assist and support where we can, there comes a point when we must address the imbalance and hold people accountable.

Ministry Burnout: A Bag We Shouldn't Carry

One of the most common bags in the church today is **ministry burnout**. How many of us are carrying roles, titles, and tasks that God never asked us to take on? We've said yes to everything because we don't want to disappoint people or because we believe "no one else will do it." But the result is a weight that slowly drains us of joy, energy, and purpose.

Moses faced this exact problem in the Old Testament. As the leader of Israel, he was overwhelmed by the constant demands of judging disputes among the people. In Exodus 18, Moses' father-in-law, Jethro, observed this and warned him, *"What you are doing is not good. You and these people who come to you will only wear yourselves out. The work is too heavy for you; you cannot handle it alone"* (Exodus 18:17–18).

Jethro's solution? Delegate. Appoint capable men to share the load. This principle applies to us today. When we try to carry everything ourselves—whether out of pride, obligation, or fear of letting others down—we're setting ourselves up for failure. God didn't design us to do it all. He created the church as a body, where each member has a role and responsibility.

The Emotional Baggage of Church Hurt

Another common bag we carry is the weight of **church hurt**. Maybe you've been wounded by gossip, criticism, or betrayal within the church. Perhaps you've given your all to a ministry, only to feel unappreciated or overlooked. These experiences leave scars, and if we're not careful, we begin to carry bitterness, resentment, or mistrust.

But what does the Bible say about these situations? Jesus Himself warns us against harboring unforgiveness. In Matthew 6:14–15, He says, *"For if you forgive other people when they sin against you, your heavenly Father will also forgive you. But if you do not forgive others their sins, your Father will not forgive your sins."*

Forgiveness doesn't mean pretending the hurt didn't happen. It means releasing the weight of it to God. When we hold onto church hurt, we're not punishing those who wronged us—we're punishing ourselves. It's like drinking poison and expecting the other person to die.

Walking on Water You Were Never Called to Walk On

There's another kind of baggage we carry—**the weight of failed attempts.** It's the burden of stepping into something that looks easy, only to realize it wasn't meant for us. In a world where success stories are constantly showcased, we're tempted to believe, *"If they can do it, so can I."* But here's the hard truth: **just because it looks easy doesn't mean it's your calling.**

Take writing a book, for example. Tools like ChatGPT have made it easier to organize thoughts, find inspiration, and streamline the writing process. But no amount of technology can replace the anointing, the calling, or the experience necessary to bring a message to life. Without the passion, the Word of God, and the fire of purpose driving you, you will find yourself burned out—trying to keep up with Peter or Paul, saying, *"I can do that too."*

Maybe you've already been there. You start something with enthusiasm, convinced you can master it like someone else did. But six months, three months—or even six weeks—down the line, you realize, *"This isn't what I love. This isn't what I've been called to do. This isn't in me."*

It's like trying to be a hairdresser when you haven't been graced for it. You step behind the chair, full of confidence, but halfway through your first treatment, you're exhausted, frustrated, and ready to sit down. That's your cue: this isn't your lane.

And yet, we keep trying to walk on water we were never meant to step on. Remember Peter? He walked on water because Jesus called him to. But what happens when we try to walk where Jesus never said, "Come"? The water doesn't hold us. It's not our calling—it's someone else's. And when we try to carry the weight of someone else's anointing, we drown under the pressure of unmet expectations, regret, and failure.

The good news? **You don't have to carry the weight of failure.** If you've found yourself drowning in regret over paths you were never meant to take, it's time to release that burden. The Bible reminds us in Psalm 37:23–24, *"The Lord makes firm the steps of the one who delights in him; though he may stumble, he will not fall, for the Lord upholds him with his hand."*

You're not meant to do everything. You're meant to do what God has called and equipped you to do. And when you walk in that calling, His grace will sustain you. If you're still carrying the weight of failed attempts, it's time to let it go and trust that God will direct your steps to solid ground.

What Are You Carrying?

So, let me ask you again: **What are you carrying, and why are you still holding onto it?**

Life is heavy enough on its own. Each day comes with its share of challenges, responsibilities, and trials. But for so many of us, no matter our station in life, we're walking around carrying more than we were ever meant to bear. And here's the thing: a lot of what's weighing us down isn't even ours.

We've picked up baggage from our children—their struggles, their mistakes, their fears. We're carrying remnants of failed relationships, holding onto bitterness, guilt, or shame. Some of us are dragging around the weight of loved ones who have passed on, unable to let go of their belongings, their debts, or the wounds they left behind.

And then there's the emotional junk. The words someone spoke over you that still ring in your ears. The trauma you've tried to bury but can't seem to escape. The mistakes you made that you replay in your mind like a broken record.

It's all in the bag.

Time to Unpack

The Bible offers us a solution to the weight we carry. In Matthew 11:28–30, Jesus invites us, *"Come to me, all you who are weary and burdened, and I will give you rest. Take my yoke upon you and learn from me, for I am gentle and humble in heart, and you will find rest for your souls. For my yoke is easy and my burden is light."*

This isn't just a comforting verse; it's a blueprint for freedom. Jesus is saying, "You don't have to carry this alone." But freedom starts with a choice. It starts with answering the question: **What are you carrying, and why are you still holding onto it?**

It's time to unpack the bags. It's time to confront the pain, the memories, and the lies that keep you bound. Together, we'll replace them with truth, hope, and the life you were meant to live.

Because you can't move forward if you're weighed down.

Chapter 1: What's in Your Bag?

Let me ask you something: What's in your bag?

No, really—have you ever stopped to think about the things you're carrying around? I'm not talking about the bag you take to work or the purse slung over your shoulder. I'm talking about the load you've been dragging through life—your emotional, mental, and even spiritual baggage.

Most of us don't even realize how heavy our bags are. We've carried them for so long, they've become a part of us. But if you were to open it up and take a good, hard look at what's inside, you might be shocked at what you find.

The Weight of the Bag Lady

Imagine the bag lady. You've seen her—she's pushing a cart overflowing with things that don't seem to belong anywhere. There's a torn shoe, a broken mirror, some mismatched socks, a cracked radio. To anyone else, it's just junk. But to her, it's life. Every item has a story, meaning, a memory

Imagine the bag lady. You've seen her—she's pushing a cart overflowing with things that don't seem to belong anywhere. There's a torn shoe, a broken mirror, some mismatched socks, a cracked radio. To anyone else, it's just junk. But to her, it's life. Every item has a story, a meaning, a memory. She clings to it all, even as it weighs her down and keeps her from moving forward.

Now, think about your own life. What's in your bag?

The Spiritual Bags We Carry

As Christians, we often carry spiritual baggage that weighs us down. Jesus addressed this directly when He said, *"Come to me, all who are weary and burdened, and I will give you rest"* (Matthew 11:28). But here's the catch: too many of us come to Him but refuse to leave our bags at His feet. We ask for rest while holding onto the very things that exhaust us.

What are some of these spiritual bags? For starters, there's **the burden of unforgiveness.** Maybe someone wronged you—deeply—and you're carrying the weight of bitterness. Ephesians 4:31–32 reminds us to *"Get rid of all bitterness, rage and anger, brawling and slander, along with every form of malice. Be kind and compassionate to one another, forgiving each other, just as in Christ God forgave you."* Yet forgiveness can feel like the heaviest bag to let go of because it demands that we release the power we think we hold over those who hurt us.

Another common spiritual weight is **the burden of self-righteousness.** We carry around our good works, our ministries, and our achievements, hoping they will prove our worthiness to God. But Isaiah 64:6 reminds us that even our most righteous acts are like filthy rags before a holy God. Our value comes not from what we do but from who we are in Christ.

Broken Mirrors

For some of us, our bag contains broken mirrors—pieces of how we once saw ourselves. Maybe there was a time when you felt confident, hopeful, and full of purpose. But something happened. Maybe someone said something cruel, or you made a mistake that you've never been able to let go of. Now, all you're left with are fragments. You keep holding onto the pieces, hoping to put them back together, but all they do is cut you every time you reach for them.

Scripture tells us that we are made in the image of God (Genesis 1:27), but life has a way of distorting that reflection. The enemy loves to shatter our sense of identity, whispering lies that we're too broken to be used by God. But the truth is, God specializes in putting broken things back together. Psalm 34:18 reminds us, *"The Lord is close to the brokenhearted and saves those who are crushed in spirit."* You don't have to carry those broken mirrors anymore; God is ready to replace them with His perfect reflection of who you are.

Torn Shoes

Others are carrying torn shoes, the evidence of the miles we've traveled and the paths we've walked. Those shoes might have served you well once, but now they're worn out, ripped, and no longer fit the journey ahead. And yet, you hold onto them because they remind you of where you've been—or because you're afraid of stepping forward into something new without them.

The Bible speaks to this idea in Isaiah 43:18–19: *"Forget the former things; do not dwell on the past. See, I am doing a new thing! Now it springs up; do you not perceive it? I am making a way in the wilderness and streams in the wasteland."* Holding onto torn shoes—whether they represent past successes or failures—can prevent us from embracing the new things God wants to do in our lives.

Cracked Radios

Then there are the cracked radios, the voices that play on repeat in your mind. Maybe it's something a parent said to you when you were a child—*"You'll never amount to anything," "You're too much,"* or *"Why can't you be more like so-and-so?"* Or maybe it's the echo of a toxic relationship, the words of someone who didn't mean you any good but left a lasting mark. Those messages might be broken and distorted, but you carry them as if they're still true, letting them shape how you see yourself and your future.

As believers, we're called to renew our minds daily (Romans 12:2). This means replacing those cracked radios with the truth of God's Word. John 10:27 says, *"My sheep listen to my voice; I know them, and they follow me."* If the voices in your mind don't align with the voice of your Shepherd, it's time to tune them out and listen to His truth instead.

Rotten Fruit

Sometimes, the things in our bag aren't just broken—they're rotten.

I remember once, I was traveling, and I grabbed some oranges to toss in my bag for the trip. I thought they'd be a nice snack if I got hungry. But after the trip, I forgot all about them. Months later, I opened the bag and was hit by the smell before I even saw it. Inside was something green, furry, and unrecognizable. For a moment, I thought something had crawled in there and died. But no—it was the oranges.

How many of us are carrying things like that? Feelings, relationships, or memories that once had purpose but have long since lost their value? Maybe it's the anger you felt after someone hurt you. At the time, it was valid—it protected you. But now it's turned into bitterness, rotting away and infecting everything around you. Or maybe it's the grief of losing someone you loved. At first, it was natural and necessary, but instead of working through it, you buried it, and now it's weighing you down in ways you can't even see.

Carrying the Weight of Failed Attempts

Another burden we often carry is **the weight of failed attempts.** This is one of the most deceptive and heavy burdens because it's tied to regret. You tried something—maybe because it looked easy or because someone else made it seem effortless—only to find out it wasn't meant for you. You poured your energy into walking a path that wasn't yours, and now you're left with frustration and a sense of failure.

Peter walked on water because Jesus called him to (Matthew 14:29). But when we step onto water without His call, it doesn't hold us. Many of us are sinking under the weight of regret, trying to walk in someone else's shoes, and wondering why we're drowning.

But failure doesn't have to define you. Proverbs 24:16 says, *"Though the righteous fall seven times, they rise again."* God's grace is sufficient to lift you up and redirect your steps when you surrender the burden of failed attempts to Him.

What Are You Carrying?

So, let me ask you again: **What's in your bag?**

Are you carrying broken mirrors, torn shoes, cracked radios, or mismatched socks? Is there rotten fruit hidden somewhere deep, something you've forgotten about but that's still taking up space? Are you dragging around words from people who never meant you any good, holding onto their weight as if it still matters? Are you burdened by the regret of failed attempts, clinging to something that was never yours to begin with?

Time to Unpack

It's time to unpack your bag. This isn't just about letting go; it's about making room for what God has for you. Hebrews 12:1 tells us, *"Let us throw off everything that hinders and the sin that so easily entangles. And let us run with perseverance the race marked out for us."*

You can't run your race if you're weighed down by baggage. You can't embrace joy if your hands are full of bitterness and regret. And you can't step into your calling if you're dragging around things God never asked you to carry.

So, take a moment and think about it. Really think. Because once you unpack it, you'll realize just how much lighter you can be.

Chapter 2: Why Are You Even Carrying That?

The Question We Avoid

Let's take a moment to really think about this: **Why are you carrying that?**

We often go through life with our bags full, weighed down by burdens that don't even belong to us. Sometimes we don't even realize it—we're just so used to carrying the load that we don't stop to ask the question: *Why am I holding this? And why was I ever given this in the first place?*

The Spiritual Perspective

The Bible provides clear guidance on the balance between helping others and taking responsibility for our own burdens. In Galatians 6:2, Paul writes, *"Carry each other's burdens, and in this way you will fulfill the law of Christ."* But just a few verses later, he says, *"For each one should carry their own load"* (Galatians 6:5). At first glance, this seems contradictory, but it's not.

The distinction lies in understanding the difference between a **burden** and a **load**. A burden is something overwhelming—a crisis, a hardship—that someone cannot bear alone. Helping someone shoulder a burden is Christlike, demonstrating compassion and love. A load, on the other hand, is the day-to-day responsibilities each person is meant to carry. If we take on someone else's load, we're not helping them; we're enabling them.

So, let's bring this back to the question: **Why are you carrying that?**

Carrying Loads That Aren't Yours

Carrying someone else's load may seem noble, kind, or even necessary. But there's a difference between helping someone carry their weight for a season and making their load your permanent responsibility.

I once saw a young man and woman, teenagers, completely in love. He adored her, and she thought he hung the moon. They were each other's first boyfriend and girlfriend, full of excitement about their new relationship. But one day, I noticed something curious. The young man was walking behind her, carrying her purse and shoes, while her hands were completely empty.

I stopped and asked him, "Why are you carrying that?"

His answer stunned me. He said, *"Because I heard something about a good man: just because a woman can carry the load, a good man would never let her."*

Now, let's pause here for a moment.

We admire the sentiment, don't we? It sounds sweet, thoughtful, even chivalrous. But let's flip the script for a second. What happens when this same dynamic plays out in other areas of life? What happens when you take on burdens that aren't yours to carry—not because someone can't carry them, but because you've convinced yourself you should?

When Good Intentions Become a Trap

Just because you can carry someone's load doesn't mean you have to.

Think about it. How often have you made yourself the answer to someone else's problem? Paying their rent, babysitting their kids, dropping everything you're doing to meet their needs. You cook their food, give them your time, and even hand over your emotional energy, all while leaving yourself drained.

When we take on responsibilities that aren't ours, we risk enabling others to remain stagnant. Jesus Himself demonstrated the importance of boundaries. In John 5, He encounters a man at the pool of Bethesda who had been an invalid for 38 years. Instead of immediately healing him, Jesus asks, *"Do you want to get well?"* (John 5:6). This question emphasizes personal responsibility. Jesus wasn't dismissive of the man's suffering, but He made it clear that the man had to participate in his own healing.

When we carry what isn't ours, we deprive others of the opportunity to grow, learn, and take ownership of their lives. Helping someone temporarily is an act of love; carrying their load indefinitely is a recipe for burnout and resentment.

Emotional Baggage Weighs the Heaviest

Sometimes, what we carry isn't physical—it's emotional. People hand us their trauma, their pain, their secrets, and we tuck them into our bags, thinking we're doing the right thing.

But here's the thing: **emotional burdens are some of the heaviest loads to carry.** You can hold someone's pain while they heal, but if you carry it too long, it becomes part of your own weight.

I've known people who've gone to jail for carrying secrets that didn't belong to them. Others have sacrificed their peace, their joy, even their mental health, because they were holding onto someone else's worry, fear, or shame.

It's one thing to be a shoulder to lean on. It's another thing entirely to become someone's permanent crutch. And while you're tossing and turning at night, weighed down by their problems, they're sleeping soundly.

The Story of Carrying Someone Else's Danger

Let me tell you a story about a young woman who learned the hard way that carrying someone else's load can come at a dangerous price.

This young lady had just graduated college and was on a celebratory trip abroad with her friends. They'd spent weeks exploring a new country, enjoying the sights, shopping, and creating memories. But as the trip came to an end, everyone was scrambling to pack their bags for the flight home.

One of her friends, someone she had trusted deeply, came to her in a panic. "I've done so much shopping," the friend said. "I don't even have room for everything I bought for my mom and my family. Can you do me a favor and carry a few of my items in your bag?"

Being a kind and helpful person, she agreed. "Of course," she said, without asking many questions. She didn't inspect the items. She didn't question why her friend was so desperate. She just wanted to help.

But at the airport, as they passed through TSA, something went terribly wrong. A dog sniffed out her bag, and the authorities pulled her aside. Confused and scared, she had no idea what was happening until the officers began questioning her. They swabbed her hands, finding traces of drugs.

Her heart sank. "This isn't mine!" she protested, her voice shaking. "I didn't pack this!"

The officers didn't believe her at first. After all, how many people claim something isn't theirs? It's a common excuse. But this time, it really wasn't hers.

What she didn't realize until that moment was that her "friend" had used her as a mule, slipping drugs into the items she had so innocently agreed to carry. The evidence was on her hands. The drugs were in her bag. Her entire future hung in the balance.

Thankfully, she told the truth. She explained exactly what had happened and identified her so-called friend as the person who had given her the items. After an investigation, the authorities cleared her name and arrested her friend. But imagine if she hadn't spoken up. Imagine if she had stayed silent out of loyalty or fear. She would have gone to jail, carrying the weight of a crime that wasn't hers.

The Lesson

Why am I sharing this story? Because so many of us are carrying things for other people that can get us into trouble.

It may not be drugs in a literal sense, but think about the emotional and spiritual baggage we take on from others. People who ask us to cover for them, lie for them, or shoulder responsibilities they don't want to face themselves. They know they're putting us in danger—risking our destiny, our peace, our reputation, and our sphere of influence—but they don't care. All they care about is finding someone else to carry the weight and take the blame.

The Power of Boundaries

Here's the truth: **not every load is yours to carry.**

Galatians 6:2 and 6:5 remind us that there's a balance between helping others and carrying our own load. Carrying burdens for others is meant to be temporary, not permanent.

Sometimes, we carry someone else's load because we don't want to say no. Other times, it's because we want to feel needed or valuable. But at the end of the day, carrying more than you're meant to only leaves you exhausted, resentful, and unable to carry your own responsibilities.

Jesus modeled boundaries throughout His ministry. He helped people, healed them, and taught them—but He also withdrew to pray, rested when He needed to, and didn't let others dictate His mission. In Luke 5:15–16, we see that even though crowds were seeking Him, Jesus often withdrew to lonely places to pray. He understood the importance of rest and refueling, and so should we.

Time to Let It Go

It's time to ask yourself some hard questions. **Is this my burden to bear?** Am I helping someone in a way that empowers them, or am I enabling them to avoid responsibility? Is this load keeping me from carrying my own purpose and joy?

Because the truth is, you can't carry someone else's load forever. At some point, you have to put it down. And when you do, you'll realize how much lighter life can be.

So, I'll ask you one more time: **Why are you even carrying that?**

Chapter 3: When the Bow Breaks

Let's Be Honest

There's only so much weight you can carry before it starts to break you down. And here's the thing: it doesn't matter how strong you are, how dedicated, or how well-intentioned—**everybody has a limit.**

For many of us, the weight we carry doesn't just come from our own responsibilities, struggles, or needs. It's compounded by the loads we take on for others. We do it out of love, obligation, or sometimes pride. We convince ourselves that we're the only ones who can handle it, that things will fall apart if we're not there to fix them. But the truth is, carrying too much for too long will destroy you—physically, emotionally, and spiritually.

When the Bow Breaks

Think about a cradle holding a baby. It's designed to support the baby's weight within reasonable limits. But what happens when you overload it? The bow—the structure that holds it all together—will break. And when the bow breaks, the cradle falls. And who suffers the most? The baby.

This is what happens in our spiritual lives when we carry too much weight, especially weight that isn't ours. That weight could be emotional, relational, or spiritual, but the principle is the same: **if you don't address the imbalance, something precious will fall, whether you want it to or not.**

It's not just the cradle that breaks. The baby—the ministry, the relationship, the business, the calling—suffers. And sometimes, that suffering can lead to death: the death of a dream, a purpose, or something precious that God entrusted to you. The bow wasn't designed to hold everything you've piled onto it. And if you don't take steps to lighten the load, the weight will inevitably cause everything to collapse.

When the bow breaks, it's not just the physical structure that fails—it's the hope, the promise, the life you were meant to nurture. **You weren't meant to carry everything, and you certainly weren't meant to carry what doesn't belong to you.** If you don't make a spiritual executive decision to put down the extra weight, the consequences can be devastating—not just for you but for everything you hold dear.

Recognizing the Weight

One of the hardest things to do is admit when the load is too heavy. Pride convinces us that we're strong enough to handle it. Obligation whispers that we *should* be able to manage it. But what we fail to recognize is that **carrying weight that isn't ours not only breaks us but can destroy the very things we've been called to protect.**

This is why it's so important to evaluate what's in your "cradle." What are you carrying? Is it your responsibility, or is it someone else's load that you've taken on? Is it something God asked you to carry, or is it something you picked up because you felt obligated?

The Danger of Carrying Too Much

Let's revisit the example of the hoarder. In Chapter 1, we talked about the woman whose home was so cluttered that she didn't even realize a cat had died under the weight of the mess. The hoarder's inability to release what wasn't serving her caused the unnecessary death of an innocent creature. The tragedy here isn't just the death of the cat—it's the fact that it could have been prevented if only the owner had recognized the weight of the problem sooner.

The same is true for us. When we carry too much—whether it's emotional baggage, unresolved conflicts, or other people's problems—we risk suffocating what's most precious. That could be your family, your health, your ministry, or your business. These things can't survive under the crushing weight of a bow that's about to snap.

The Spiritual Perspective

The Bible speaks to the importance of recognizing our limits. In Matthew 11:28–30, Jesus invites us, *"Come to me, all who are weary and burdened, and I will give you rest. Take my yoke upon you and learn from me, for I am gentle and humble in heart, and you will find rest for your souls. For my yoke is easy and my burden is light."*

Notice that Jesus doesn't say, "Carry it all yourself." Instead, He offers a partnership. His yoke is easy because He shares the weight. But too often, we resist that invitation. We convince ourselves that we're strong enough to manage on our own, and we end up overwhelmed and exhausted.

The Baby in the Cradle

Imagine a mother carrying her newborn in a cradle. She knows the cradle is precious and fragile, and she treats it with care. But what if she starts adding things to the cradle that don't belong there? Bags of groceries, books, or even heavy stones. At first, the cradle holds. But over time, the weight becomes too much, and the bow snaps.

Now, who suffers? Not the mother. Not the cradle. It's the baby—the precious life entrusted to her care—that takes the fall.

This is what happens when we allow the weight of unnecessary burdens to overload our lives. It might be a ministry God gave you, a business you started, or a relationship you're nurturing. Whatever it is, **when the bow breaks, the thing you were meant to protect will suffer.** And sometimes, it's not just hurt—it's irreversible damage.

The Warning Signs

God is always faithful to warn us when we're carrying too much. But the question is, are you listening?

- Are you constantly tired, yet unwilling to ask for help?
- Are you irritable with your loved ones because you're overwhelmed?
- Are you losing your joy in the things you once felt called to do?
- Are you struggling to spend time with God because you're too busy carrying everything else?

These signs aren't meant to shame you—they're God's way of saying, *"You're carrying more than you were meant to. Come to Me. Let Me help."*

When the Bow Breaks in Ministry

This principle applies especially in ministry. Too many of us take on roles and responsibilities that weren't meant for us, either because we want to help or because we're afraid to say no. But when we overload ourselves, the ministry—the "baby" in the cradle—suffers.

Consider Moses in Exodus 18. He was trying to judge all the disputes of the Israelites on his own. The weight of responsibility was overwhelming, but he didn't realize it until his father-in-law, Jethro, confronted him. Jethro said, *"What you are doing is not good. You and these people who come to you will only wear yourselves out. The work is too heavy for you; you cannot handle it alone"* (Exodus 18:17–18).

Moses listened to Jethro's advice and delegated responsibilities to capable men. By lightening his load, he was able to focus on what God had called him to do, and the people's needs were still met.

The Cost of Ignoring the Weight

But what happens when you refuse to listen? When you keep carrying more and more, ignoring the signs? Eventually, the bow breaks, and the consequences can be devastating.

You might lose your health. Stress and exhaustion take their toll on your body, leading to sickness or burnout.

You might lose your peace. Carrying too much weight leaves you emotionally depleted and spiritually distant from God.

Worst of all, you might lose what matters most. Your family, your ministry, your relationships—these precious things suffer when you're overloaded and overwhelmed.

Putting Down the Weight

The good news is, it's not too late to put the weight down.

Jesus said, *"Come to me, all who are weary and burdened, and I will give you rest."* That invitation is for you. God never designed you to carry everything on your own. He's asking you to trust Him with the things you can't handle.

So, what's in your cradle? What weight have you added that doesn't belong there?

Take a moment to evaluate your life. Identify the things that are causing strain—the unnecessary burdens, the extra weight—and make a spiritual executive decision to let them go. It might be hard, and it might upset some people, but protecting what God has entrusted to you is worth it.

The Choice Is Yours

If you don't lighten the load, the bow will break. And when it does, the things you care about most will suffer. But if you choose to trust God, to set boundaries, and to release what isn't yours to carry, you'll find freedom, peace, and strength.

It's not too late to save the cradle—and the baby inside.

It's Time

It's time to stop carrying weight that isn't yours. It's time to trust God with the things that are too heavy for you. And it's time to protect what matters most before the bow breaks.

Because when the bow breaks, everything falls.

But it doesn't have to.

Chapter 4: Who Packed Your Bag?

Let's Pause for a Moment:

Let's pause for a moment and ask a simple but profound question: **Who packed your bag?**

Think about it—how often do we carry things in life that we didn't pack for ourselves? Responsibilities, opinions, guilt, shame, expectations—all stuffed into the pockets of our emotional and spiritual luggage by others, leaving us with a load that's far too heavy. And yet, instead of questioning it, we haul it around, breaking our backs under the weight of things that were never meant for us to carry.

The Overstuffed Bag

I remember a time when my husband was preparing for a trip. He was clear about his limits: the airline allowed a 25-pound bag, and he needed to keep things light so he could travel easily. But in my mind, I thought, *He's going to need this and that. What if this comes up? I'd better make sure he's prepared.*

So, the night before, I quietly started adding to his bag. Heavy shoes, a laptop, chargers, an extra outfit—everything I thought he might need. I stuffed things into the pockets, tucked items into corners, and zipped it all up.

The next morning, as he lifted the bag, he paused. "Honey," he said, "did you add something to this bag? It feels heavier."

I laughed nervously, *"Oh, just a few things!"*

He sighed but didn't say much. It wasn't until he got to the airport and tried to lift the bag onto the scale that he realized the problem. The bag was over the weight limit. He had to make adjustments right there at the counter, pulling things out, rearranging, and deciding what to leave behind.

How often does this happen in life? People start packing your bag for you, adding things here and there—sometimes with good intentions, sometimes not—and before you know it, you're carrying a load that's far too heavy.

Carrying What Others Pack for You

Sometimes, the people in our lives are like me in that story—adding to your bag because they think they know what's best. They fill your bag with:

- **Opinions:** "You should do it this way." "This is what's expected of

you."
- **Responsibilities:** "You can handle it—you always do."
- **Judgments:** "Why didn't you do more?" "I wouldn't have let them treat me that way."
- **Emotional Baggage:** "Hold onto this anger for me." "Can you carry my guilt for a while?"

At first, it may not seem like much. But over time, the weight adds up. And here's the thing—while others may have good intentions, **they don't know what you can handle. Only you know your limits.**

The TSA Checkpoint: Whose Bag Is This?

Have you ever been at the airport and watched someone get stopped at the TSA checkpoint? The agent pulls the bag aside, points to the conveyor belt, and says, *"Whose bag is this?"*

The owner has to step forward, raise their hand, and take responsibility for the contents.

Then comes the inspection. If the bag contains prohibited items—liquids over the limit, something too heavy, or something unsafe—the agent gives the traveler two options:

1. Leave the item behind and continue to your destination.
2. Stay behind with the baggage.

This is a picture of life. God has destinations He wants to take us to, but many of us are being held up at the "security checkpoint" because our bags are too heavy. **We're carrying things that don't meet His standards for the journey.**

Boundaries: Saying No to What Others Pack

Here's the truth: **you have the power to decide what goes into your bag.** Just because someone tries to hand you their burdens, their opinions, or their responsibilities doesn't mean you have to take them.

Think about what Jesus said in Matthew 11:28–30:

"Come to me, all who are weary and burdened, and I will give you rest. Take my yoke upon you and learn from me, for I am gentle and humble in heart, and you will find rest for your souls. For my yoke is easy, and my burden is light."

Notice that He doesn't tell you to take on everyone else's yoke. He says to take His yoke—a light and manageable one.

The gift of saying **no** is a boundary that protects you from carrying what others try to pile on you. **No** is a complete sentence. You don't need to explain it, justify it, or feel guilty for saying it.

As an evangelist once said, this is the season to stand your ground and say, *"No, that's enough."* It's not about being mean or dismissive—it's about knowing your limits and refusing to let someone else overload you.

If they push back, take your time and say, *"Which part of 'no' don't you understand? The N or the O? Let me know, and I'll break it down for you."*

The Risks of Carrying Too Much

When you allow others to pack your bag, you risk:

1. **Missing Your Destination:** Like the TSA example, you can't board the plane if your bag is too heavy. In life, you may miss opportunities, blessings, or peace because you're weighed down.
2. **Losing Your Strength:** Carrying too much will exhaust you. You'll find yourself breaking under the pressure, unable to carry even the things that truly matter.
3. **Neglecting Your Purpose:** When your energy is spent on everyone else's baggage, there's little left for your own calling and responsibilities.

Unpacking and Letting Go

So, whose bag is this? **Who packed it?** It's time to unpack everything and decide what stays and what goes.

Ask yourself these questions:

- Does this belong to me, or was it handed to me by someone else?
- Is this helping me get where I'm going, or is it holding me back?
- Does this align with my purpose, or is it a distraction?

Remember, just because someone hands you something doesn't mean you have to take it. And if you've already taken it, you can always hand it back.

Lighten the Load

God has a destination for you, but you can't get there if your bags are overloaded. It's time to let go of the guilt, the shame, and the responsibilities that were never yours in the first place.

Take inventory of your life. Unpack the bag. And the next time someone tries to hand you something, pause and ask yourself, *Is this mine to carry?* If it's not, hand it back with love and keep moving forward.

Because the lighter your load, the easier it is to reach your destination.

The Weight You Didn't Realize You Were Carrying

Sometimes, we're carrying things that we didn't even realize had been packed into our bag. Words spoken over us in childhood—labels like "not good enough," "too sensitive," or "failure"—can stay buried deep in the corners of our emotional luggage. These words, though spoken long ago, still weigh us down, shaping how we see ourselves and limiting how far we're willing to go.

Think back to your own life. What labels, expectations, or burdens have you been carrying without even realizing it? Maybe someone told you that you wouldn't amount to much, and now you overcompensate, trying to prove them wrong. Or maybe someone expected you to be the "strong one" in your family, and now you carry the unspoken pressure to hold everything together—even when it's breaking you apart.

The Power of Awareness

The first step to lightening your load is awareness. You have to take the time to unpack your bag, examine its contents, and identify what doesn't belong there. This requires intentionality and honesty—two things that are often uncomfortable but absolutely necessary.

Start by asking yourself these questions:

1. **Who told me I needed to carry this?**
   Was it a parent, a friend, a boss, or even society? Identify the source of the expectation or responsibility.
2. **Is this weight helping me or hindering me?**
   Some things are worth carrying, like love, compassion, and accountability. But if the weight is rooted in guilt, shame, or fear, it's time to let it go.
3. **What does God say about this?**

Align what you're carrying with the Word of God. If it doesn't align, it's not meant for you. Remember Matthew 11:30: *"For my yoke is easy, and my burden is light."*

Repacking with Purpose

Once you've unpacked your bag and laid everything out, it's time to repack with purpose. Think about what truly matters, what aligns with your values and calling, and what will help you reach your destination.

Here's how you can repack intentionally:

- **Keep what nourishes you.** Carry the things that bring you closer to God, deepen your relationships, and help you grow.
- **Leave behind what drains you.** Say goodbye to unnecessary guilt, shame, and the expectations of others that don't serve your purpose.
- **Trust God with the rest.** You don't have to figure everything out on your own. Leave space in your bag for grace, peace, and the unknown.

A Practical Example

Let's bring this concept into real life with a practical example. Imagine you've been asked to join a committee at your church. You already have a full plate—work, family, personal commitments—but you feel pressured to say yes because you don't want to disappoint anyone.

Before you automatically agree, pause. Take a moment to unpack the "why" behind your decision. Are you saying yes because you genuinely feel called to serve in this way, or are you saying yes because you're afraid of what people will think if you say no?

If it's the latter, consider this: saying yes to something that doesn't align with your purpose means saying no to something that does. It might mean saying no to rest, no to time with your family, or no to the things God is calling you to prioritize.

Give yourself permission to say no. Remember, as we said earlier, **no is a complete sentence.**

Freedom in Letting Go

When you release the things you were never meant to carry, you'll experience a freedom you didn't know was possible. You'll feel lighter, more focused, and more aligned with God's purpose for your life.

Psalm 55:22 reminds us, *"Cast your cares on the Lord and he will sustain you; he will never let the righteous be shaken."* This is an invitation to release the weight, to trust God with your burdens, and to walk in the freedom He has for you.

A New Way to Travel

Imagine walking through life with a bag that's perfectly packed—not overstuffed, not too heavy, but just right. Every item in the bag has a purpose. Every pocket is organized. You know exactly what you're carrying and why.

This is the kind of freedom God wants for you. He doesn't want you dragging around a bag filled with things that don't serve you. He wants you to travel light, unburdened, and free to focus on the journey ahead.

The Final Question

So, let me ask you one last time: **Who packed your bag?**

If it's full of things that aren't yours—burdens, expectations, responsibilities, or labels—it's time to unpack, let go, and repack with intention. Don't let the weight of someone else's baggage hold you back from the life God has planned for you.

Because the truth is, you can't move forward if you're weighed down by what doesn't belong to you.

Chapter 5: Are You a Bag Lady or a Mr. Bojangles?

A Question of Perspective

When you think of a "bag lady," the image is often specific. You picture a woman pushing a cart, her life's belongings piled high in bags, dragging the weight of her world behind her. But here's a question: **What if it's not about gender? What if it's about mindset?**

The truth is, there are "bag people" of all kinds. Some might look more like a Mr. Bojangles—dragging their pain, grief, and burdens behind them, wearing a brave face but barely holding it together inside. Being a "bag lady" or a "Mr. Bojangles" has nothing to do with whether you're male or female—it's about what you're carrying and why.

The Story of Mr. Bojangles

One of the ways we explored this idea was by reflecting on the song *Mr. Bojangles*. If you've ever listened to the lyrics, it tells the story of a man who carried so much grief and pain that it shaped his entire life. He lost his only companion, his dog, and his world seemed to stop. In his pain, he turned to dancing as a way to cope.

But here's the heartbreaking part: **no one cared about his story.** All they wanted was the performance. They weren't interested in what he was carrying or why; they just wanted him to entertain them and then disappear.

How many of us live like that? Carrying the weight of our own pain and burdens, only to have people ignore what we're going through and expect us to keep "dancing"?

Carrying Burdens for Others

I once conducted an exercise at church that opened everyone's eyes. I asked my team to scatter random items—pillows, bags, toys, cups, you name it—all over the sanctuary. When people arrived, their reactions varied.

- Some people walked in and didn't even notice the mess. They just kicked things out of their way and kept going.
- Others were visibly annoyed, looking around with disgust but not doing anything to address it.

- And then there were a few who walked in and immediately started picking things up, asking, *"What's going on here?"*

The truth is, **people handle burdens the same way.** Some don't notice. Some are annoyed but leave it for someone else to handle. And some will try to take on everything, even if it's not their responsibility.

Which one are you?

Emotional Dumpsters

Let's get real: some people will treat you like a dumpster.

They come to you with all their frustrations, their anger, their emotional mess. They unload on you—every worry, every grudge, every heartbreak—and when they're done, they walk away feeling lighter. But what about you?

You're left holding all their mess. You might feel physically sick, your stomach in knots, or emotionally drained. Their burdens have become yours, and they've left you with the stench of everything they dumped.

Have you ever been in a bathroom where someone left a mess? You flush it and leave, but the smell lingers. That's what it's like when someone dumps their emotional junk on you—it lingers, weighing you down long after they've gone.

Who's Responsible for Your Bag?

Here's the truth: **people will only pack your bag if you let them.**

The Bible reminds us in Proverbs 4:23: *"Above all else, guard your heart, for everything you do flows from it."* Guarding your heart means setting boundaries. It means saying no when someone tries to add their junk to your load.

Sometimes, you have to stop and say:

- "No, I'm not going to sit and gossip with you."
- "No, you can't unload your anger on me every time someone makes you mad."
- "No, I'm not a garbage can for your negativity."

Saying no is a complete sentence. It's not selfish; it's self-preservation. If someone asks why, you can say, *"Because my bag is full."*

Lessons from TSA: Lighten Your Load

When you fly, the Transportation Security Administration (TSA) has strict rules about what you can bring. If your bag is too heavy or contains items that aren't allowed, they'll pull you aside and ask, *"Whose bag is this?"*

You have to raise your hand and take responsibility. Then, they give you two options:

1. Leave the item behind and continue to your destination.
2. Stay behind with your baggage.

The same is true in life. If you're carrying something that's not allowed—guilt, shame, unforgiveness, bitterness—you have to decide whether to leave it behind or let it keep you from moving forward.

God has destinations for you, but you can't board the plane if your load is too heavy. Sometimes, you need to unpack the bag, let go of the unnecessary, and trust Him to take you where you're meant to go.

The Weight of Misplaced Responsibility

How often do we pick up things that don't belong to us? Maybe it's because we feel obligated. Maybe it's because we think we're helping. Or maybe we've been conditioned to believe that saying no makes us selfish.

But misplaced responsibility is dangerous. It not only exhausts you but also prevents the person who *should* be carrying the load from growing. Galatians 6:2 tells us to *"Carry each other's burdens,"* but Galatians 6:5 reminds us that *"each one should carry their own load."* There's a difference between helping someone temporarily and carrying what was never yours to bear.

When you take on what isn't yours, you're not helping—you're enabling.

It doesn't matter if you're a woman or a man—being a "bag person" is about mindset, not gender. **We all have the capacity to carry too much,** to hold onto things that don't serve us, and to allow others to pile their junk on us.

Some of us are like the "Bag Lady," weighed down by years of emotional clutter—grudges, regrets, and unhealed wounds. Others are like Mr. Bojangles, masking our pain with performance, dancing for the approval of others while breaking under the weight of our own grief. And many of us are both, juggling the chaos of emotional baggage while trying to meet the demands of others.

The question is: **When will you put the bag down?**

Recognizing the Signs
How do you know if you're carrying too much? Here are a few warning signs:

1. **You're constantly tired.** Not just physically, but emotionally and spiritually. You feel like no matter how much sleep you get, you can't recharge.
2. **You're irritable or short-tempered.** The smallest inconveniences set you off because you're already running on empty.
3. **You're avoiding people.** You find yourself withdrawing, not because you don't care, but because you can't handle one more conversation or responsibility.
4. **You're losing your joy.** The things that once brought you happiness—your family, your work, your ministry—now feel like a chore.

These signs are God's way of nudging you to stop, reflect, and lighten your load. Ignoring them will only lead to burnout or breakdown.

How Others Add to Your Bag
People add to your bag in different ways:

- **Guilt:** "If you loved me, you'd do this for me."
- **Shame:** "You should've done more. You're not enough."
- **Control:** "Let me tell you how you should handle this."
- **Dependency:** "I can't do this without you."

It's easy to fall into the trap of thinking you're helping by taking on these burdens. But the reality is, you're only making the problem worse—for them and for yourself. **You can't save everyone, and you weren't meant to.**

Unpacking the Bag
So, how do you unpack what's been weighing you down? It starts with taking an honest inventory.

1. **Identify what's in your bag.** Write it down if you need to. What are the burdens you're carrying? Whose problems, expectations, or responsibilities have you taken on?

2. **Ask yourself if it belongs to you.** Is this something God has called you to carry, or did someone else pack it for you?
3. **Decide what to let go of.** Some things need to be handed back to their rightful owner. Others need to be given to God entirely.

In 1 Peter 5:7, we're reminded to *"Cast all your anxiety on him because he cares for you."* This isn't just a suggestion—it's an invitation. God is saying, *"You don't have to carry this alone. Give it to Me."*

The Cost of Carrying Too Much

When you refuse to let go, the cost is high.

- **Your Health:** Stress and exhaustion take a toll on your body. Headaches, back pain, insomnia—these are all signs that your load is too heavy.
- **Your Relationships:** When you're overburdened, you have less patience and energy for the people who matter most. Your family often gets the leftovers of your time and attention.
- **Your Purpose:** Carrying unnecessary baggage distracts you from the things God has called you to do. You can't fully step into your purpose if you're weighed down by things that aren't yours to carry.

The Power of "No"

One of the most liberating things you can do is learn to say no.

Saying no doesn't make you selfish—it makes you wise. It's a boundary that protects your energy, your peace, and your purpose. Even Jesus set boundaries. In Mark 1:35–38, after a long night of healing and ministering to people, Jesus withdrew to a solitary place to pray. When His disciples found Him and told Him everyone was looking for Him, He said, *"Let us go somewhere else—to the nearby villages—so I can preach there also. That is why I have come."*

Jesus knew His mission, and He didn't let others dictate how He spent His time. You can follow His example by staying focused on what God has called you to do and saying no to distractions.

Moving Forward

As we move into the next chapter, we'll start exploring what it means to clean it up. But before you can begin that process, you need to answer some hard questions:

- Who packed your bag?
- What are you carrying that doesn't belong to you?
- Are you letting others treat you like a dumpster?

Because the truth is, **you can't move forward until you unpack what's weighing you down.**

Time to Lighten Your Load

God has a destination for you, but you can't get there if your bags are overloaded. It's time to let go of the guilt, shame, and unnecessary responsibilities that were never yours to carry. Take inventory of your life, unpack the bag, and start fresh.

The next time someone tries to hand you their baggage, remember this: **Not every load is yours to bear.** Say no, set boundaries, and trust God to carry what you can't.

Because the lighter your load, the easier it is to move forward.

Chapter 6: Burdens of Legacy: When the Weight Transfers

The Weight of Generational Expectations

Imagine you're carrying a bag, and every time someone from your family's past hands you a responsibility, you add it to your load. Maybe it's a family business, cultural tradition, or even unspoken expectations. Over time, the weight becomes heavier and harder to carry. You might not even realize it, but you're hauling not just your own burdens but also those passed down from generations before you.

Legacy is a beautiful concept. It's about passing something meaningful from one generation to the next—a dream, a business, a tradition, or a blessing. But what happens when legacy becomes a burden instead of a gift?

The Turkey Legs Story

There's a famous story about a woman who would always cut the legs off her turkey before roasting it. One day, her daughter asked her why she did this. She shrugged and said, "I don't know. My mother always did it." Curious, the daughter went to her grandmother and asked the same question. The grandmother laughed and replied, "Honey, we only cut the legs off the turkey because our roasting pan was too small! You don't need to do that anymore."

For generations, this family wasted perfectly good turkey legs simply because no one stopped to ask, "Why do we do this?"

This story illustrates how traditions, habits, and burdens can be passed down without question. What may have made sense at one time can become a meaningless or even harmful weight when circumstances change.

Cultural and Family Baggage

Let's take this idea a step further with a real-life example. A young man moved to America to pursue his education. His family worked tirelessly to send him to college, laboring in their home country to fund his dream. After graduating, he got married and started a family, but the expectations from his family back home didn't stop. They insisted that he send a portion of his income back to the village every month.

At first, he felt obligated. After all, they had sacrificed so much for him. But over time, the financial strain started affecting his new family. His wife became resentful, their bills piled up, and he found himself unable to save for their future. Despite his efforts, the weight of his family's expectations grew heavier. When he tried to set boundaries, his family accused him of being ungrateful.

This is what happens when legacy turns into a burden. The young man wanted to honor his family, but the cost was too high—it almost destroyed his marriage and his mental health.

The Balance Between Honor and Boundaries

The Bible teaches us to honor our parents (Exodus 20:12), but it also emphasizes the importance of setting healthy boundaries. In Luke 14:26, Jesus said, *"If anyone comes to me and does not hate father and mother, wife and children, brothers and sisters—yes, even their own life—such a person cannot be my disciple."* This doesn't mean we should literally hate our family, but it does highlight the need to prioritize God's calling above all else.

The young man's story teaches us that honoring others doesn't mean sacrificing ourselves entirely. It's about finding a balance—acknowledging the sacrifices made by previous generations while also recognizing our own limits.

Generational Baggage vs. Generational Blessing

Generational baggage often stems from unresolved trauma, unspoken expectations, or outdated traditions. Here are some examples:

- **Emotional Baggage:** Unresolved family conflicts that create cycles of bitterness or resentment.
- **Cultural Baggage:** Expectations to adhere to traditions that no longer serve a purpose.
- **Spiritual Baggage:** Legalistic views of faith passed down without understanding God's grace.

On the flip side, generational blessings can be just as powerful:

- **Financial Legacy:** Inheriting resources or knowledge that empower future generations.
- **Spiritual Legacy:** Passing down a strong foundation of faith and

prayer.
- **Cultural Legacy:** Celebrating traditions that bring joy and connection.

The key is to discern which parts of our legacy are worth carrying forward and which need to be released.

Breaking the Cycle

If you've recognized generational baggage in your own life, here are steps to break the cycle:

1. **Ask Questions:** Take a closer look at family traditions, expectations, and habits. Ask, "Why do we do this? Is it still necessary?"
2. **Heal the Root:** If the baggage comes from unresolved trauma, seek healing through therapy, prayer, or counseling.
3. **Set Boundaries:** Communicate your limits with love and clarity. For example, "I value what you've done for me, but I need to focus on my own family now."
4. **Create New Patterns:** Replace outdated traditions or harmful habits with meaningful, intentional practices.

Proverbs 13:22 says, *"A good person leaves an inheritance for their children's children."* This inheritance isn't just about money—it's about leaving behind a legacy of freedom, faith, and purpose.

When Legacy Becomes a Choice

Let's look at two examples of how legacy can be either embraced or rejected:

1. **Toys "R" Us:** For generations, this iconic brand was a place where children's dreams came alive. The founders envisioned it as a lasting legacy for their children and grandchildren. But when the next generation inherited the company, they lacked the passion to sustain it. They chose to let it go, and the business folded.
2. **Marvel Comics:** Stan Lee poured his heart into creating a world of superheroes, but after his passing, his daughter sold the rights. She chose to move on rather than carry the weight of her father's legacy.

Neither decision was necessarily wrong—it simply shows that legacy must align with the values and desires of those who inherit it. If it doesn't, it becomes a burden instead of a blessing.

Spiritual Legacy: Passing on Freedom, Not Baggage

From a spiritual perspective, the best legacy we can leave is one rooted in God's love and grace. Here are ways to ensure your legacy blesses future generations:

1. **Live with Integrity:** Show your children and grandchildren what it means to walk in faith and freedom.
2. **Teach with Intention:** Pass down not just rules but understanding—why you believe what you believe and how it applies to their lives.
3. **Release Control:** Trust God to guide the next generation, even if they choose a different path.

Closing Thoughts

Legacy is a powerful force. It can shape families, communities, and futures. But if we're not intentional, it can also become a weight that crushes instead of empowers. By setting boundaries, breaking cycles, and focusing on freedom, we can transform generational baggage into generational blessings.

As you reflect on your own life, ask yourself:

- What am I carrying that doesn't belong to me?
- How can I honor my past while protecting my future?
- What kind of legacy do I want to leave behind?

Because the truth is, the legacy you pass on is up to you.

Chapter 7: Forgiving Others, Forgiving Yourself

The Weight of Unforgiveness

Imagine carrying a bag filled with stones, each one representing a grudge, a wound, or a regret. At first, you may not notice the weight. But as time passes, the load becomes heavier, affecting your ability to move forward. This is what unforgiveness does—it weighs us down, ties us to the past, and prevents us from living freely.

Jesus spoke plainly about forgiveness. In Matthew 6:14–15, He said, *"For if you forgive other people when they sin against you, your heavenly Father will also forgive you. But if you do not forgive others their sins, your Father will not forgive your sins."* Forgiveness is not just a nice idea; it's a command that brings healing and freedom.

But what happens when the person you need to forgive is yourself?

The Silent Burden of Self-Unforgiveness

Many of us are quick to forgive others but struggle to extend that same grace to ourselves. We replay our mistakes, failures, and regrets, asking, *How could I have let this happen? How could I have been so blind?* This self-directed blame can become one of the heaviest burdens we carry.

Take the story of the young man who sent money back to his family's village. He wanted to honor their sacrifices, but the financial strain affected his own family. When he could no longer pay his visa fees, the guilt was overwhelming. His wife's frustration only added to his internal torment. He began to question everything, blaming himself for every misstep.

This cycle of guilt and regret often leads to feelings of worthlessness. We think, *If I had been smarter, stronger, or more disciplined, I wouldn't be in this mess.* But the truth is, no one is perfect, and God's grace covers all our shortcomings.

Forgiving Others: Setting the Prisoner Free

Unforgiveness is often described as drinking poison and expecting the other person to suffer. It doesn't hurt them—it hurts you. Holding onto resentment keeps you tied to the offense and the offender, robbing you of peace and joy.

Forgiving someone doesn't mean excusing their behavior or pretending it didn't happen. It means choosing to release them into God's hands. Romans 12:19 reminds us, *"Do not take revenge, my dear friends, but leave room for God's wrath, for it is written: 'It is mine to avenge; I will repay,' says the Lord."*

Forgiveness is about setting yourself free. It's saying, *I refuse to let this person or this situation control me any longer.*

Steps to Forgiveness

If you're struggling to forgive someone, here are some practical steps:

1. **Acknowledge the Hurt:** Be honest about what happened and how it affected you. Suppressing your pain only prolongs the healing process.
2. **Pray for Strength:** Ask God to help you release the offense. Forgiveness is a spiritual act that requires divine assistance.
3. **Let Go of Revenge:** Release the need to get even. Trust that God will handle justice in His way and His timing.
4. **Choose to Forgive:** Forgiveness is a choice, not a feeling. Even if your emotions don't immediately align, your decision to forgive starts the process.

Self-Forgiveness: Releasing Yourself

Forgiving yourself can be even more challenging than forgiving others. It requires confronting your own mistakes, owning your actions, and choosing to let go of guilt and shame.

Self-forgiveness doesn't mean ignoring or excusing your behavior. It means accepting God's grace and moving forward in freedom. 1 John 1:9 reminds us, *"If we confess our sins, He is faithful and just to forgive us our sins and to purify us from all unrighteousness."*

Here's how to start the process of forgiving yourself:

1. **Confess and Repent:** Acknowledge your mistakes before God and ask for His forgiveness. Trust that His grace is sufficient.
2. **Reject the Lies:** The enemy loves to whisper lies like, *You'll never be good enough,* or, *God can't forgive you for this.* Replace these lies with the truth of Scripture.
3. **Extend Grace to Yourself:** If God, who knows all, has forgiven you,

why are you holding yourself to a higher standard?
4. **Focus on Growth:** Learn from your mistakes and use them as stepping stones toward becoming the person God has called you to be.

A Prayer for Self-Forgiveness

If you're struggling to forgive yourself, pray this prayer:

"Lord, I come before You with the weight of my mistakes. I confess that I've allowed guilt and shame to rule my heart, and I've carried burdens You never intended for me. Today, I choose to forgive myself, just as You have forgiven me. I release the blame, the regret, and the bitterness I've held against myself. Help me walk in freedom and grace, trusting in Your mercy. In Jesus' name, Amen."

Therapy and Emotional Healing

For many, the weight of unforgiveness—whether toward others or oneself—requires more than prayer alone. Therapy can be a valuable tool for unpacking unresolved emotions and processing trauma. It doesn't replace faith but works alongside it, providing practical strategies for healing.

In some cultures, therapy is still stigmatized. Phrases like, *What happens in this house stays in this house*, have silenced generations of pain. But God calls us to live in truth and freedom, not secrecy and shame. Proverbs 11:14 says, *"Where there is no guidance, a people falls, but in an abundance of counselors there is safety."*

Seeking therapy is not a sign of weakness—it's an act of courage.

Generational Baggage: Breaking the Cycle

Unforgiveness isn't just a personal issue—it's often passed down through generations. When we don't heal, our pain seeps into the lives of those around us, especially our children.

Consider the story of the woman who cut the turkey legs. This harmless tradition might seem trivial, but it represents a larger truth: we often perpetuate behaviors without questioning their origins. When those behaviors are rooted in trauma or bitterness, they can become generational baggage.

To break the cycle:

1. **Identify the Baggage:** Reflect on the patterns or behaviors in your

family that no longer serve a purpose.
2. **Seek Healing:** Address unresolved wounds through therapy, prayer, or counseling.
3. **Create New Traditions:** Replace old patterns with practices that promote freedom, joy, and connection.

Freedom Through Forgiveness

When we forgive—both others and ourselves—we create space for God's peace to fill our hearts. Matthew 11:28–30 reminds us that Jesus offers rest for the weary. But to receive that rest, we must be willing to release what's weighing us down.

Reflection Questions

1. Who do you need to forgive, and why?
2. What lies have you believed about yourself that need to be replaced with God's truth?
3. What steps can you take today to begin the process of self-forgiveness?

Closing Thoughts

Forgiveness is a journey, not a one-time event. It requires courage, grace, and faith. But the reward is freedom—a lighter load, a clearer path, and a heart aligned with God's will.

Take the first step. Let go of the weight. Forgive others. Forgive yourself. And step into the life God has prepared for you.

Chapter 8: The Lighter Load

What Does Freedom Feel Like?

Imagine standing at the top of a hill after a long, exhausting climb. The air is fresh, the view is breathtaking, and for the first time in a long while, you can breathe deeply. That's what freedom feels like when you release the burdens you were never meant to carry. It's a feeling of lightness, clarity, and peace.

But here's the truth: many of us have carried our burdens for so long that we can't even imagine life without them. The weight has become part of who we are. We don't know what it's like to live lightly because we've never experienced it—or if we have, we've forgotten.

In Matthew 11:28–30, Jesus says, *"Come to me, all who are weary and burdened, and I will give you rest. Take my yoke upon you and learn from me, for I am gentle and humble in heart, and you will find rest for your souls. For my yoke is easy, and my burden is light."*

These verses remind us that we were never meant to carry the weight alone. Jesus invites us to exchange our heavy burdens for His lighter yoke. But what does that look like in everyday life?

Letting Go of the Heavy Load

Letting go of burdens is not a one-time event—it's a continual process of surrender. Every day, we must examine what we're carrying and decide what to keep and what to release.

Here are some steps to start lightening your load:

1. **Identify the Weight:** Take inventory of your emotional, spiritual, and relational burdens. What's weighing you down? Is it guilt, shame, unforgiveness, or the expectations of others? Write it down.
2. **Release What's Not Yours:** Just because someone handed you a burden doesn't mean you have to carry it. Ask yourself, *Is this my responsibility?* If not, let it go.
3. **Trust God with the Rest:** There are some burdens you can't carry, even if they are yours. Trust God to help you with these. Surrender them to Him in prayer.

Gratitude as a Tool for Freedom

One of the most effective ways to lighten your load is to practice gratitude. Gratitude shifts your focus from what you lack to what you have. It changes your perspective, reminding you of God's goodness even in the midst of challenges.

Philippians 4:6–7 says, *"Do not be anxious about anything, but in every situation, by prayer and petition, with thanksgiving, present your requests to God. And the peace of God, which transcends all understanding, will guard your hearts and your minds in Christ Jesus."*

When you focus on gratitude, you'll notice that some of the burdens you've been carrying start to feel lighter. Why? Because gratitude reminds you that you're not alone—God is with you, providing for you every step of the way.

The Benefits of Living Lightly

What happens when you let go of unnecessary burdens and embrace a lighter load? The benefits are transformative:

1. **Emotional Freedom:** You no longer feel weighed down by guilt, shame, or regret. Your heart feels lighter, and your mind is clearer.
2. **Spiritual Growth:** With fewer distractions, you can focus more on your relationship with God. You hear His voice more clearly and align your life with His purpose.
3. **Health and Wellness:** Emotional and spiritual burdens often manifest physically. Releasing them can lead to better sleep, reduced stress, and improved overall health.
4. **Deeper Relationships:** When you're not consumed by your own weight, you have more energy to invest in your relationships.

Modern-Day Challenges: Social Media and Comparison

In today's world, one of the heaviest burdens we carry is the pressure to compare ourselves to others. Social media, while a powerful tool for connection, often becomes a source of discontent. We scroll through highlight reels of other people's lives, feeling inadequate in comparison.

But here's the truth: no one's life is as perfect as it appears on social media. The Bible warns against comparison in 2 Corinthians 10:12: *"When they measure themselves by themselves and compare themselves with themselves, they are not wise."*

To lighten the load of comparison, consider these steps:

- **Limit Your Time Online:** Set boundaries for how much time you spend on social media.
- **Focus on Your Journey:** Remember that God has a unique plan for your life.
- **Practice Gratitude:** Reflect on the blessings in your own life instead of envying others.

Building Habits for a Lighter Life

Living lightly requires intentionality. Here are some habits to help you sustain freedom from unnecessary burdens:

1. **Daily Surrender:** Start each day by surrendering your burdens to God. Pray, *"Lord, I give you this day and everything it holds. Help me to carry only what you've called me to."*
2. **Regular Reflection:** Set aside time each week to evaluate what you're carrying. Ask yourself, *Is this still mine to carry?*
3. **Healthy Boundaries:** Learn to say no when necessary. Protect your time, energy, and peace.
4. **Community Support:** Surround yourself with people who encourage and uplift you. Share your burdens with trusted friends or mentors.
5. **Stay in the Word:** Let scripture guide you and remind you of God's promises.

Stepping Into Your Purpose

When you let go of the weight, you create space for God to move in your life. You're no longer consumed by distractions or tied down by unnecessary burdens. Instead, you're free to focus on His calling and purpose for you.

Ephesians 2:10 says, *"For we are God's handiwork, created in Christ Jesus to do good works, which God prepared in advance for us to do."* God has a plan for your life, but you can't fulfill it if you're weighed down by things He never intended for you to carry.

Reflection Questions

1. What burdens are you carrying that you need to release?
2. How does practicing gratitude shift your perspective on your challenges?
3. What steps can you take today to live more lightly?

Prayer for a Lighter Load

"Lord, I come to You weary and burdened. I surrender the weight I've been carrying—the guilt, the shame, the expectations, and the responsibilities that aren't mine. Teach me to trust You with my burdens and to carry only what You've called me to. Help me to live lightly, with joy and peace, as I walk in Your purpose. In Jesus' name, Amen."

Closing Thoughts

Living lightly isn't just about letting go—it's about stepping into the freedom and purpose God has for you. When you release the weight, you'll find that life is not only lighter but also richer, fuller, and more aligned with God's will.

The lighter load is available to you today. All you have to do is let go.

Chapter 9: A Framework for Freedom

Laying Down the Weight

Freedom is not a destination; it's a process. For many of us, the idea of freedom feels distant, almost unattainable. We've carried burdens for so long—baggage from past mistakes, broken relationships, unfulfilled dreams, and even the expectations of others—that we can't imagine what life without those weights would look like. But here's the truth: God's design for you is freedom. He doesn't want you to live bound by chains, whether emotional, spiritual, or relational. He wants you to walk in the fullness of His grace, healing, and purpose.

In John 8:36, Jesus declares, *"So if the Son sets you free, you will be free indeed."* This is the foundation of freedom: understanding that it's already yours through Christ. The challenge, however, is learning to live in that freedom daily.

The First Step: Taking Inventory

Before you can release the weight, you need to identify what you're carrying. This process is like cleaning out a closet—you have to take everything out, examine it, and decide what to keep and what to let go.

Ask yourself:

- What burdens am I carrying that don't belong to me?
- Which weights have been handed to me by others?
- Are there lies I've believed about myself that need to be replaced with God's truth?
- What relationships, habits, or responsibilities are draining me instead of strengthening me?

Taking inventory requires honesty and courage. It's not easy to confront the things that have kept you bound, but it's the first step toward freedom.

Returning the Weight

Once you've identified the burdens you're carrying, the next step is to return them to their rightful owner. Not every weight you carry is yours to bear. Some of it belongs to other people—family, friends, colleagues—and some of it belongs to God.

In 1 Peter 5:7, we're instructed to *"Cast all your anxiety on Him because He cares for you."* This means trusting God with the things you can't control and refusing to carry burdens that aren't meant for you.

Returning the weight might look like:

- Setting boundaries with people who rely on you for things they should handle themselves.
- Surrendering your worries to God through prayer.
- Letting go of guilt or shame for things that are beyond your control.

The Power of Forgiveness

Forgiveness is one of the most powerful tools for releasing weight. Whether it's forgiving someone who hurt you or forgiving yourself for mistakes you've made, forgiveness breaks the chains that keep you tied to the past.

Matthew 6:14–15 reminds us, *"For if you forgive other people when they sin against you, your heavenly Father will also forgive you. But if you do not forgive others their sins, your Father will not forgive your sins."*

Forgiveness is not about excusing the wrongs done to you; it's about choosing to let go of the hold they have on your life. It's about freeing yourself from the bitterness, resentment, and pain that weigh you down.

If you're struggling with forgiveness, start small:

1. Acknowledge the hurt and how it affected you.
2. Pray for the strength to forgive, even if your feelings don't immediately align.
3. Release the offense into God's hands, trusting Him to bring justice and healing.

Reframing Your Mindset

True freedom begins in the mind. Romans 12:2 instructs us to *"Be transformed by the renewing of your mind."* This transformation happens when we replace the lies we've believed with the truth of God's Word.

Here are some common lies and the truths that counter them:

- **Lie:** "I'll never be enough."
  Truth: *"I am fearfully and wonderfully made" (Psalm 139:14).*
- **Lie:** "I have to carry this on my own."
  Truth: *"Come to me, all who are weary and burdened, and I will give you rest" (Matthew 11:28).*
- **Lie:** "My past defines me."
  Truth: *"Therefore, if anyone is in Christ, the new creation has come: The old has gone, the new is here!" (2 Corinthians 5:17).*

To reframe your mindset, make a habit of declaring these truths over your life. Write them down, meditate on them, and speak them aloud when the lies try to creep back in.

Building a Framework for Freedom

Living in freedom requires intentionality. Here are practical steps to build a framework for freedom in your life:

1. **Daily Surrender:** Begin each day by surrendering your burdens to God. Pray, *"Lord, I give You this day. Help me to carry only what You've called me to, and to trust You with the rest."*
2. **Set Boundaries:** Learn to say no without guilt. Protect your time, energy, and peace by setting limits with others.
3. **Surround Yourself with Support:** Freedom is easier to maintain when you're part of a community that encourages and uplifts you. Seek out friends, mentors, or church groups who align with God's purpose for your life.
4. **Stay in the Word:** Scripture is your foundation for freedom. Let it guide your decisions, renew your mind, and remind you of God's promises.
5. **Celebrate Progress:** Freedom is a journey, not a destination. Celebrate the small victories along the way, and give yourself grace when you stumble.

Freedom and Purpose

When you release the weight, you create space for God to move in your life. You're no longer consumed by burdens that drain you. Instead, you're free to focus on the purpose God has for you.

Ephesians 2:10 says, *"For we are God's handiwork, created in Christ Jesus to do good works, which God prepared in advance for us to do."* God has specific plans for your life, but you can't fulfill them if you're weighed down by things He never intended for you to carry.

Freedom isn't just about feeling lighter; it's about stepping into the fullness of who God created you to be. It's about using your gifts, talents, and experiences to make an impact in the world.

Reflection Questions

1. What burdens are you carrying that don't belong to you?
2. How can you take inventory of your life and identify the weights you need to release?
3. What steps will you take to build a framework for freedom in your daily life?

A Prayer for Freedom

Heavenly Father,

I come to You today with the burdens I've been carrying, many of which were never mine to bear. Lord, I surrender them to You now. I trust You to take the weight off my shoulders and to guide me toward freedom. Help me to forgive those who have hurt me and to release the pain, resentment, and bitterness that have kept me bound. Teach me to forgive myself, Lord, and to walk in the truth of Your grace and love.

Father, I declare that I am no longer defined by my past, my mistakes, or the expectations of others. I am defined by Your love and Your purpose for my life. Help me to set healthy boundaries, to renew my mind with Your Word, and to surround myself with people who encourage and uplift me. Lord, I choose freedom today. I choose to walk in the fullness of Your promises, trusting that You have good plans for me. Thank You for breaking every chain and giving me the courage to move forward. In Jesus' name, Amen.

Closing Thoughts

Freedom isn't a destination; it's a journey. It's a daily decision to let go of what's weighing you down and to trust God with every step. As you continue this journey, remember that freedom isn't just for you—it's for everyone your life will touch. By walking in freedom, you become a beacon of hope and light to those still struggling under the weight.

Embrace the process. Celebrate the progress. And never forget that the lighter load is not just possible—it's promised.

Chapter 10: The Takers and the Broken

Mr. Bojangles: A Story of Brokenness

There was a pastor who owned more than 20 houses, each one a potential source of income and influence. This pastor surrounded himself with people who were skilled, loyal, and, most importantly, broken. Among them was a man I'll call "Joe," a carpenter who joined the church after his wife passed away. Brokenhearted and searching for purpose, Joe moved to the state and quickly became invaluable to the pastor, helping renovate and rebuild his properties.

Joe was skilled, diligent, and desperate for a fresh start. After completing renovations on the pastor's 20th property, Joe asked for pay to enroll in truck-driving school—a dream he had long nurtured to begin a new chapter of his life. The pastor, knowing how much he depended on Joe, promised to provide the funds. But the promise was never fulfilled.

The pastor had no intention of letting Joe go. He wasn't just a worker; he was the pastor's free maintenance man. To keep him close, the pastor manipulated Joe's brokenness. He knew Joe had once struggled with alcoholism, and instead of encouraging his sobriety, the pastor exploited his vulnerability. At a dinner with church staff, the pastor ordered Joe a drink, making it appear harmless. Slowly but surely, the pastor enticed Joe back into the addiction he had worked so hard to escape.

The Manipulation of Brokenness

Joe, desperate for a new life, began to demand the money he was promised. Instead of paying him, the pastor would bring expensive bottles of cognac and gin, ensuring Joe remained functional but broken. Joe would sober up just long enough to finish work on the houses before falling back into despair. The more Joe drank, the more verbally belligerent he became. He showed up to church drunk, broken, and confused, while the pastor dismissed his behavior as grief over his wife's passing.

The pastor knew the truth but preferred Joe broken. Why? Because broken people are easier to control. They're easier to keep in one place, reliant on the crumbs of help you throw their way. The pastor didn't want Joe to succeed. He didn't want him to find healing. He wanted him just sober enough to be useful and just broken enough to be dependent.

When People Prefer You Broken

What do you do when the people you trust want you to stay broken? This is a hard truth: there are those who thrive on your dysfunction. They don't want you healed because your healing disrupts their comfort. Your freedom makes them uncomfortable. Your success makes them irrelevant.

In Mark 5, we read the story of a man possessed by a legion of demons. The people of his city were content as long as he stayed among the tombs, cutting himself and crying out in torment. But when Jesus healed him, casting the demons into a herd of pigs, the townspeople were angry. They begged Jesus to leave their region.

Why? Because the man's healing disrupted their system. They were comfortable with his brokenness—it fit their expectations and didn't challenge their way of life. But his healing was a threat.

How many people in your life are content as long as you stay in the graveyard, cutting yourself emotionally, spiritually, or physically? How many are happy to see you poor, depressed, or struggling—as long as you're still useful to them?

The "Cheers" Effect

There's a danger in becoming addicted to being needed for your brokenness instead of your purpose. It's the "Cheers" effect—the desire to go where everyone knows your name, even if they only know you for your dysfunction. When people applaud you for being a victim, you might start to settle into that identity. But God didn't create you to be defined by your wounds. He created you to walk in wholeness and purpose.

Joe's story is a warning. When you realize people are more comfortable with your brokenness than your healing, it's time to step away. The pastor in Joe's life was more than willing to exploit him for what he was good at while ignoring what God had called him to be.

Exploitation in Disguise

We live in a world where acts of kindness can often be manipulated for public recognition. You've likely seen social media videos where someone helps a homeless person, records the interaction, and shares it online. While some of these actions come from a place of genuine compassion, others are performative. Their goal isn't to help but to gain likes, shares, and applause.

The same can happen in spiritual spaces. Some people claim to offer help, but their motives are selfish. They want to keep you broken because it makes them look better.

Beware of those who publicize their kindness to you. While there are genuine helpers, there are also takers—people who give just enough to maintain control over your life. Be discerning.

Divine Interventions and Destiny Helpers

Sometimes, brokenness feels overwhelming. But God has a way of stepping in and sending the right people at the right time—people who don't exploit your pain but remind you of who you were created to be. These "destiny helpers" may not always look the way you expect, but they are sent to help you move forward.

Think of the viral videos where someone gives a homeless person a haircut, a shave, and a new outfit. The transformation brings the person to tears—not because of the material change, but because they see a glimpse of who they used to be. This is what true kindness looks like—helping someone see their God-given worth.

Pray for divine intervention in your life. Ask God to send people who will help you heal, grow, and fulfill your purpose.

Are You a Mr. Bojangles or a Bag Lady?

Joe's story reflects the heart of this book. Are you a Mr. Bojangles—broken, crying, and being exploited by people who prefer you that way? Or are you a Bag Lady—pushing around burdens that don't even belong to you?

Maybe you're both. But regardless of where you find yourself, the question remains: Will you choose healing, or will you stay in the graveyard?

A Call to Prayer

Let's pray together for freedom and healing:

"Lord, I come to You as I am—broken, burdened, and in need of Your touch. I ask You to remove the people in my life who exploit my pain and replace them with

destiny helpers who will lead me toward healing and purpose. Help me to see myself as You see me, not defined by my wounds but by Your love. I release every burden, every lie, and every chain that has kept me bound. Lord, transform me and show me who I was created to be. In Jesus' name, Amen."

Closing Reflection

Joe's story is a warning and an invitation. It warns us to be cautious of those who prefer our brokenness and challenges us to step into the healing God offers. Don't settle for being needed for what you're good at when God has called you to something greater.

Are you ready to lay down the bags and leave the graveyard? Are you ready to see yourself as God sees you? Because healing isn't just possible—it's promised.

Self-Analysis: Identifying the Weight

Chapter 1: What's in Your Bag?

1. What does "baggage" represent in the context of the book?
   a) Physical luggage
   b) Emotional, spiritual, and relational burdens
   c) Unnecessary belongings
   d) Career challenges
2. Why do people often carry emotional baggage?
   a) They enjoy the weight.
   b) They don't realize they're carrying it.
   c) It's part of their physical routine.
   d) It's required by society.
3. What is the first step to addressing the weight you carry?
   a) Ignoring it
   b) Identifying it
   c) Sharing it with others
   d) Giving it away
4. In the Bible, Matthew 11:28-30 speaks about Jesus offering what to the weary?
   a) A heavier burden
   b) Rest and a lighter load
   c) Wealth and success
   d) Friendship

Chapter 2: Why Are You Even Carrying That?

1. What often leads people to carry responsibilities that aren't theirs?
   a) Pride
   b) Guilt or obligation
   c) Lack of strength
   d) Competition
2. What does Galatians 6:2 encourage believers to do?
   a) Carry others' burdens temporarily.
   b) Take on everyone's load permanently.
   c) Avoid helping others at all.
   d) Keep all burdens to yourself.
3. Why is setting boundaries important when helping others?
   a) It protects both parties from burnout.
   b) It ensures complete dependency.
   c) It allows others to avoid responsibility.
   d) It prevents growth in relationships.
4. What is one practical way to stop carrying unnecessary burdens?
   a) Continue saying yes to everything.
   b) Identify what's yours and let go of the rest.
   c) Never offer help again.
   d) Ignore others' problems entirely.

Chapter 4: Who Packed Your Bag?

1. What is the main question asked in this chapter?
   a) How heavy is your bag?
   b) Who packed your bag?
   c) Where did you get your bag?
   d) What color is your bag?
2. What is a key sign that someone else is packing your bag?
   a) You feel completely in control.
   b) You're unaware of the burden until it becomes overwhelming.
   c) The bag feels light and manageable.
   d) The burden brings you joy.
3. What is the lesson of the TSA metaphor in this chapter?
   a) Security checks are inconvenient.
   b) You must take responsibility for what's in your bag.
   c) It's best to carry everything for others.
   d) TSA always lightens the load for travelers.
4. What does Proverbs 4:23 teach about guarding your heart?
   a) Avoiding unnecessary emotions
   b) Protecting yourself from carrying unnecessary burdens
   c) Keeping your heart from loving others
   d) Eliminating all responsibilities

Chapter 5: Bag Lady, Mr. Bojangles, or Both?

1. The story of Mr. Bojangles highlights which emotional challenge?
   a) Overworking to succeed
   b) Performing for others while hiding pain
   c) Traveling too much
   d) Ignoring professional responsibilities
2. How does mindset play a role in the burdens we carry?
   a) It dictates whether we see the weight as a challenge or a choice.
   b) Mindset has no effect on burdens.
   c) A positive mindset eliminates all burdens.
   d) Mindset creates physical weight.

3. What societal expectation often burdens men more than women?
   a) Managing the household
   b) Being the sole provider
   c) Taking care of children
   d) Performing at church
4. What is one way to stop "performing" for others' approval?
   a) Seek validation from others.
   b) Confront and release the need for external affirmation.
   c) Focus on improving your performance.
   d) Avoid relationships entirely.

Chapter 7: Forgiving Others, Forgiving Yourself

1. Why is forgiveness essential to letting go of burdens?
    a) It sets both you and others free.
    b) It allows you to control the situation.
    c) It ensures the other person apologizes.
    d) It creates distance between people.
2. What does Matthew 6:14-15 teach about forgiveness?
    a) Forgiveness is optional.
    b) Forgiving others allows God to forgive you.
    c) Forgiveness should be earned.
    d) Forgiveness applies only to small issues.
3. What often prevents self-forgiveness?
    a) Lack of personal responsibility
    b) Belief that we don't deserve grace
    c) Dependence on others' approval
    d) Complete denial of wrongdoing
4. What practical tool is suggested for self-forgiveness in the book?
    a) Ignoring past mistakes
    b) Journaling and prayer
    c) Seeking more responsibilities
    d) Focusing on others' mistakes

Final Review

1. How does releasing baggage impact your ability to fulfill God's purpose?
   a) It frees you to focus on what matters most.
   b) It increases your workload.
   c) It removes all responsibility.
   d) It leads to financial success.
2. What is one practical step to prevent carrying unnecessary weight in the future?
   a) Refuse to help others entirely.
   b) Say "yes" to everything and figure it out later.
   c) Set healthy boundaries and re-evaluate them regularly.
   d) Only take on tasks that bring personal benefit.
3. What is the ultimate goal of the book?
   a) To help readers live with fewer burdens and more freedom in Christ.
   b) To encourage people to avoid all responsibility.
   c) To focus solely on forgiveness.
   d) To eliminate challenges altogether.

Answer Key 1

1. b
2. b
3. b
4. b
5. b
6. a
7. a
8. b
9. b
10. b
11. b
12. b
13. b
14. a
15. b
16. b
17. a
18. b
19. b
20. b
21. a
22. c
23. a

This multiple-choice quiz tests understanding while encouraging reflection. It balances factual recall with application and interpretation of the lessons in your book. Let me know if you'd like to expand the number of questions or customize further for specific themes!

Chapter 8: The Lighter Load

1. What does Jesus promise to those who come to Him with their burdens (Matthew 11:28-30)?
   a) Eternal suffering
   b) Rest and a lighter yoke
   c) Recognition and rewards
   d) Wealth and prosperity
2. Why is it important to let go of unnecessary baggage?
   a) It helps maintain control over others.
   b) It creates space for joy, peace, and purpose.
   c) It ensures others depend on you.
   d) It guarantees success in all areas of life.
3. How does gratitude help lighten your emotional load?
   a) It shifts focus from lack to abundance.
   b) It makes others appreciate you more.
   c) It removes all challenges.
   d) It forces you to ignore problems.
4. What habit can help sustain a lighter load?
   a) Saying yes to every opportunity
   b) Regularly evaluating what's in your "bag"
   c) Carrying others' responsibilities
   d) Avoiding personal reflection
5. How does living lightly align with God's purpose for us?
   a) It frees us to focus on His calling and serve others joyfully.
   b) It eliminates all challenges in life.
   c) It allows us to avoid responsibilities.
   d) It ensures we are always in control.

Chapter 9: A Framework for Freedom

1. What is the first step in releasing burdens according to the book?
   a) Ignoring them
   b) Identifying the weight you're carrying
   c) Blaming others for the weight

d) Pretending the weight isn't there
2. Why is it important to "return the weight to its rightful owner"?
   a) It teaches others to take responsibility for their own load.
   b) It eliminates relationships with others.
   c) It ensures you never help anyone again.
   d) It avoids conflict.
3. How does forgiveness fit into the framework for freedom?
   a) It is optional depending on the burden.
   b) It releases bitterness and creates space for healing.
   c) It benefits the other person more than yourself.
   d) It delays the healing process.
4. Why is emotional healing described as a continual process?
   a) Life consistently presents new challenges and burdens.
   b) Healing only happens in rare circumstances.
   c) Once healed, no further effort is needed.
   d) It requires avoidance of emotional triggers.
5. What role does prayer play in maintaining freedom from baggage?
   a) It keeps you dependent on others.
   b) It connects you to God's strength and guidance.
   c) It eliminates all future burdens.
   d) It ensures you never need therapy.
6. What is the ultimate goal of living free from unnecessary weight?
   a) To live selfishly and avoid responsibilities.
   b) To embrace joy, purpose, and alignment with God's will.
   c) To seek validation from others.
   d) To avoid all challenges in life.

Forgiveness and Emotional Healing

1. What is the key reason self-forgiveness is important?
   a) It ensures others will respect you.
   b) It allows you to move forward without guilt or shame.
   c) It helps you control situations.
   d) It makes others forgive you too.
2. What is a practical step suggested for self-forgiveness?

a) Journaling and prayer
b) Focusing on others' mistakes
c) Avoiding personal reflection
d) Relying on external validation
3. How can therapy and prayer work together in emotional healing?
a) Therapy addresses emotional patterns, and prayer strengthens spiritual alignment.
b) Therapy replaces the need for prayer.
c) Prayer eliminates the need for therapy.
d) Both are independent of each other.
4. Why is therapy often stigmatized in some cultures?
a) It's seen as unnecessary for Christians.
b) Cultural norms prioritize silence over vulnerability.
c) There's a belief that "what happens in this house stays in this house."
d) All of the above.
5. How does Matthew 18:21–22 challenge traditional views of forgiveness?
a) By encouraging forgiveness "seventy times seven," it emphasizes unlimited grace.
b) It suggests forgiveness only for minor offenses.
c) It implies forgiveness must be earned.
d) It limits forgiveness to one instance per person.
6. Why does unforgiveness often feel like carrying a heavy weight?
a) It ties you emotionally to the offense and the offender.
b) It forces others to feel guilty.
c) It provides a sense of control.
d) It eliminates emotional attachment.

Generational Baggage

1. What does generational baggage refer to?
a) Material possessions inherited from family
b) Emotional and spiritual burdens passed down from one generation to the next
c) Legal responsibilities within families

d) The weight of managing a family business
2. How can traditions become generational baggage?
   a) When their purpose is no longer relevant but continues out of habit
   b) When they are meaningful and bring joy
   c) When they help strengthen family bonds
   d) When they are adapted to new circumstances
3. What is the first step to breaking generational cycles of baggage?
   a) Ignoring the cycle
   b) Questioning the origins of traditions or habits
   c) Continuing the traditions without question
   d) Confronting family members aggressively
4. How does legacy shift from a burden to a blessing?
   a) When it aligns with God's purpose and the recipient's calling
   b) When it requires no effort or responsibility
   c) When it is passed on without communication
   d) When it focuses solely on financial inheritance
5. Why is communication essential in passing down a legacy?
   a) It helps ensure alignment between generations.
   b) It eliminates misunderstandings.
   c) It prevents burdensome expectations.
   d) All of the above.

Modern-Day Burdens

1. How does social media add to emotional baggage?
   a) By fostering comparison and validation-seeking
   b) By improving mental health
   c) By encouraging authenticity
   d) By limiting external influences
2. What role does therapy play in addressing the baggage of modern challenges?
   a) It provides tools for processing emotions and setting boundaries.
   b) It replaces the need for spiritual growth.
   c) It eliminates burdens permanently.
   d) It makes challenges disappear immediately.
3. How can gratitude combat the overwhelm caused by modern life?
   a) By focusing on abundance instead of comparison
   b) By ignoring challenges
   c) By emphasizing external validation
   d) By reducing responsibilities
4. What does Romans 12:2 suggest about dealing with societal pressures?
   a) Conform to expectations for better acceptance.
   b) Be transformed by renewing your mind.
   c) Avoid change entirely.
   d) Seek validation from others.
5. What is the ultimate purpose of addressing all forms of baggage?
   a) To live lightly and fulfill God's purpose for your life
   b) To eliminate all challenges
   c) To seek constant validation
   d) To gain worldly success

Answer Key 2

1. b
2. b
3. a
4. b
5. a
6. b
7. a
8. b
9. a
10. b
11. b
12. b
13. a
14. a
15. d
16. a
17. a
18. b
19. a
20. b
21. a
22. d
23. a
24. a
25. a
26. b
27. a

Closing Prayer: A Cry for Freedom and Healing

ABBA Father, You are the God of endless mercy, grace, and compassion. Your Word declares in Lamentations 3:22–23, *"Because of the Lord's great love we are not consumed, for His compassions never fail. They are new every morning; great is Your faithfulness."* Father, I stand in awe of the endless flow of Your mercy, available to me even in my unworthiness.

Today, I lift every **Bag Lady** and **Mr. Bojangles**, every soul weighed down by pain, burdens, and brokenness, before Your throne. I declare that every limitation, every shackle, and every yoke of bondage in their lives is shattered by the authority of the name of Jesus. Lord, Your Word reminds us in Philippians 2:10 that *"at the name of Jesus, every knee shall bow, in heaven and on earth and under the earth."* Father, let every knee of affliction, stagnation, addiction, and delay bow before You today, in Jesus' name.

Heavenly Father, Your Word declares in 1 Corinthians 6:19, *"Do you not know that your bodies are temples of the Holy Spirit, who is in you, whom you have received from God? You are not your own."* I boldly proclaim that every person carrying the weight of broken marriages, lost dreams, or unfulfilled potential is Your ark—a carrier of Your divine presence. Therefore, every spiritual or emotional dragon assigned against their progress, destiny, and purpose must fall and die in the name of Jesus.

Lord, I cry out for the freedom of those who feel exploited, abandoned, or trapped in cycles of despair. Just as the **man with a legion of demons** found freedom and purpose when You intervened, I pray that You would break every chain of oppression and every stronghold of addiction. Your Word in Psalm 68:1 says, *"May God arise, may His enemies be scattered; may His foes flee before Him."* Father, arise! Scatter every power of darkness contending with the purpose of Your children. Let no **Bag Lady** or **Mr. Bojangles** remain confined to their brokenness.

Mighty God, You are Jehovah Rapha, the Lord who heals. I declare by faith that every voice of infirmity—whether physical, emotional, or spiritual—speaking against Your children is silenced now in the mighty name of Jesus. Isaiah 53:5 proclaims, *"By His stripes we are healed."* Let Your healing power flow now, bringing restoration to body, mind, and soul. Father, I speak to every wound, every scar, and every memory carried by the **Bag Ladies** and **Mr. Bojangles** in our midst. Heal them, Lord. Let them see themselves as You see them—whole, beloved, and purposed for greatness.

I prophesy divine health, peace, and freedom over Your children. Sickness shall no longer have dominion over them. Lord, let Your miracle power overshadow every person carrying the baggage of chronic pain, terminal disease, generational affliction, or emotional torment. By the power in the name of Jesus, healing is our portion.

ABBA Father, You are the God of breakthrough, and I call upon You to intervene in every area of delay, stagnation, and hopelessness. Your Word declares in Jeremiah 29:11, *"For I know the plans I have for you, declares the Lord, plans to prosper you and not to harm you, plans to give you hope and a future."* Father, I decree that every **Bag Lady** and **Mr. Bojangles** who has carried the weight of others' expectations, wounds, or broken systems will see their long-awaited breakthrough manifest now by fire, in the name of Jesus.

Lord, I pray for those who have settled for being needed for their brokenness rather than stepping into the purpose You designed for them. Help them see that they are more than their pain, more than their skills, and more than what others expect of them. Remind them, Lord, that they are Your masterpiece, created for good works (Ephesians 2:10).

Father, I declare today that:

- Every **Bag Lady** pushing around the weight of broken families, careers, and lives will find freedom.
- Every **Mr. Bojangles** who has danced for the approval of others will stop performing and step into their God-given identity.
- Every person who feels unseen, unheard, and undervalued will encounter Your presence in a transformative way.

ABBA Father, arise and let Your light shine in the darkest places of their hearts. Send destiny helpers—people with pure motives, who will lift them up rather than exploit their pain. And for those who have felt used or betrayed, teach them to forgive, to heal, and to trust in You again.

Thank You, Lord, for being the God who turns mourning into dancing, ashes into beauty, and brokenness into purpose. I seal this prayer in the mighty name of Jesus, declaring that freedom, healing, and breakthrough are ours.

Amen.

Dear Reader, Thank You for Investing in yourself!

Thank you for taking this journey with me. Whether you came across it by recommendation, curiosity, or divine appointment, I believe this book was meant to be a part of your journey.

This work represents not just my words but my heart, my experiences, and my prayers. As you turned these pages, I hope you found yourself reflected in the stories, challenges, and victories shared within. Each chapter was written with you in mind—to encourage you, uplift you, and help you let go of the baggage that may have weighed you down for far too long.

To every **Bag Lady** or **Mr. Bojangles** who has carried the weight of life's burdens, my prayer is that this book gave you a glimpse of freedom, a whisper of hope, and a reminder of your God-given worth. You are more than the pain you've endured, and you are not alone in your struggles.

If this book spoke to you, if it stirred something in your spirit or encouraged you to let go of the weight, I invite you to share it with someone who may need the same encouragement. Freedom is not meant to be kept—it's meant to be shared.

May God continue to bless you, heal you, and guide you into the fullness of His purpose for your life.

With gratitude,

Apostle

Don't miss out!

Visit the website below and you can sign up to receive emails whenever Apostle Paula Ferguson publishes a new book. There's no charge and no obligation.

https://books2read.com/r/B-A-EDXVD-ODUVI

BOOKS2READ

Connecting independent readers to independent writers.

Did you love *Bag Ladies & Mr. Bojangles: Spiritual Vagabonds in the Church*? Then you should read *Arsenal: Prayers Declarations and Decrees That Will Move Heaven and Shake Hell*[1] by Apostle Paula Ferguson!

In an age where darkness assaults every stronghold—families torn by division, finances gripped by scarcity, and souls entangled by unseen forces—*Arsenal: Prayers, Declarations, and Decrees That Will Move Heaven and Shake Hell* by Apostle Paula Ferguson emerges as a divine imperative, a sacred armory that is not an option but a **REQUIREMENT** for every believer. This is no ordinary book; it is a celestial war chest, an apostolic mandate wielding 323 Spirit-breathed proclamations to dismantle strongholds, restore legacies, and align earth with Heaven's glory. Your victory will not come by wishful thinking; it will only come by decree! Open your mouth and SPEAK!

Forged under Apostle Ferguson's apostolic anointing, shaped by her mentors—Apostle Craig Ferguson, her steadfast husband; Denise Michelle Ray, her intercessor; Apostle Douglas Dwayne Rudd Sr., her spiritual father; Prophet

---

1. https://books2read.com/u/bQz9gd

2. https://books2read.com/u/bQz9gd

Lovy L. Elias, her prayer mentor; and Prophetess Taryn Nicole Bishop, her spiritual mother—*Arsenal* equips you with precision across 18 battlegrounds, from *Family Restoration* to the groundbreaking *Technological Warfare and Protection*. Rooted in over 150 Scriptures, each decree is a divine edict. Proclaim, "I decree that my marriage is fortified by divine love" (Chapter 1, #7), and watch unity prevail. Declare, "I decree that no algorithm invades my destiny" (Chapter 11, #16), and see God's shield rise. Whether a new believer sowing faith or a prayer general commanding Heaven's armies, this book is your non-negotiable weapon to co-create with God.

Apostle Ferguson's testimony—miracles of healed bodies, shifted policies, transformed lives—infuses *Arsenal* with unyielding power. Uniting African, Hispanic, Asian, and global believers, it transcends cultures in a universal call to arms. Morning Warfare Prayer Points and a Scripture Index ensure daily conquest, while vivid metaphors—your voice as a divine scepter, decrees as heavenly prescriptions—make truth accessible. This book is a **REQUIREMENT** to stand as a joint-heir with Christ (Romans 8:17), wielding your tongue's power (Proverbs 18:21) to break chains and spark revival. You cannot face this hour unarmed. Embrace *Arsenal*. Move Heaven. Shake Hell.

Read more at www.fosaservices.com.

Also by Apostle Paula Ferguson

Arsenal: Prayers Declarations and Decrees That Will Move Heaven and Shake Hell
Fridge, Forks, and Fresh Starts: Building a Healthy Kitchen
Arsenal: Prayers, Declarations, and Decrees for the Family That Will Move Heaven and Shake Hell
Bag Ladies & Mr. Bojangles: Spiritual Vagabonds in the Church

Watch for more at www.fosaservices.com.

About the Author

Apostle Paula Ferguson is a dynamic prophetic leader, teacher, and author with decades of ministry experience, dedicated to empowering believers to walk boldly in their God-given authority. Known for her profound spiritual insight and unwavering commitment to biblical truth, she equips the body of Christ to break strongholds, shift atmospheres, and manifest God's promises through faith-filled declarations. Her ministry is marked by testimonies of healing, deliverance, and restoration, as she guides others to align their lives with Heaven's purposes.

As the author of *Bag Lady, Mr. Bojangles: It's Time to Let It Go, Make It Make Sense*, and *I Just Don't Feel Like It! Finding Motivation When Life Hits Snooze*, Apostle Paula combines real-life stories, scriptural wisdom, and practical steps to inspire transformation. She describes herself as a "human computer," receiving divine downloads from God to navigate life's challenges, a testimony woven throughout her writings and teachings.

Married to her best friend and greatest supporter, Apostle Craig Ferguson, she serves alongside him to foster spiritual growth, emotional healing, and holistic wellness. Together, they empower individuals to recognize their worth in Christ and embrace their divine purpose. Apostle Paula's transparent, compassionate approach and apostolic anointing make her a trusted voice for those seeking to move heaven and shake hell.

Read more at www.fosaservices.com.

About the Publisher

FOSA Publishing LLC—short for *Family of Successful Authors*—is dedicated to empowering writers from all backgrounds to bring their stories to life. While our roots are in Christian publishing, we proudly support authors of diverse genres and messages.

Inspired by stories of perseverance, we aim to support authors in publishing their messages quickly and effectively. Our encouragement is simple: start where you are, trust your vision, and let us help you bring it to life.

Join our family of successful authors—your voice deserves to be heard.

Read more at https://fosaservices.com/.

www.ingramcontent.com/pod-product-compliance
Lightning Source LLC
Chambersburg PA
CBHW022109160426
43198CB00008B/409